THE FACTS ABOUT

Police, People and Power

by Paul Almonte
and Theresa Desmond

CRESTWOOD HOUSE

New York

Maxwell Macmillan Canada
Toronto

Maxwell Macmillan International
New York   Oxford   Singapore   Sydney

LIBRARY OF CONGRESS CATALOGING-IN-PUBLICATION DATA

Almonte, Paul.
   Police, people and power / by Paul Almonte &
Theresa Desmond. — 1st ed.
     p.   cm. — (The Facts about)
Includes glossary/index.
   Summary: Examines the problems that can occur in determining a balance
between the actions of police in apprehending criminals and the rights of
individual citizens.
   ISBN 0-89686-748-X
   1. Police—Juvenile literature. 2. Police—United States—Complaints
against—Juvenile literature. 3. Civil rights—United States—Juvenile
literature. [1. Police—Complaints against. 2. Civil rights.] I. Desmond,
Theresa. II. Title. III. Title: Police, people and power. IV. Series: Facts
about.
HV7922.A46   1992
363.2′3′0973—dc20   91-46951

PHOTO CREDITS

cover: Richard Bachmann
Richard Bachmann: 4, 8, 10, 14, 18, 21, 23, 26–27, 31, 34, 36, 39, 41, 44
Linda Harris: page 46

CRESTWOOD HOUSE

Crestwood House
Macmillan Publishing Company
866 Third Avenue
New York, NY 10022

Maxwell Macmillan Canada, Inc.
1200 Eglinton Avenue East
Suite 200
Don Mills, Ontario M3C 3N1

Macmillan Publishing Company is part of the Maxwell Communication Group of Companies.

First edition
Printed in the United States of America

10 9 8 7 6 5 4 3 2 1

CONTENTS

SUNDAY IN THE PARK

Seventeen-year-old Eric Morales clearly remembers the last time he and his friends went to the neighborhood park. He was sitting on a cement wall, having a cigarette. As he and his friends talked and laughed, they suddenly noticed two police officers strolling toward them. One of the cops was swinging his nightstick.

"Good evening, gentlemen," one of the officers said.

Eric and his friends looked back at the police officers without saying anything.

"A report just came in over the radio. Some young men just grabbed a woman's purse a couple of blocks from here," the cop continued. "You boys wouldn't know anything about that, would you?"

"No," Eric said quickly, "we wouldn't."

The other police officer walked up to Eric until he was only a few inches from Eric's face.

"You know," the cop said, looking down into Eric's eyes, "I don't think I like your attitude."

Eric stared back at him. "And I don't like yours, either," he replied.

Suddenly the cop thrust his nightstick against Eric's chest, pushing him back. "Listen, 'Julio,'" he said to Eric, "let's get something straight. I know that you and

Often black and Hispanic teenagers believe that they are unjustly harassed by the police because of their skin color.

5

your little friends think you can get away with anything. But now you have to deal with me. And I'm gonna be on your back night and day just so that little old lady who lost her purse can sleep at night. You got it?" He poked the nightstick at Eric's chest one last time before he and his partner strolled away.

For Eric, this incident is only one of the ways he thinks his rights as a citizen are not being respected. He and his friends are constantly harassed by the police. They are stopped, questioned or simply watched all the time.

Eric believes that because he is Hispanic, and a teenager, the police automatically suspect him. He says the police have no right to stop him when he's minding his own business. He and his friends distrust the police. They say that instead of protecting them, the police are there only to harass them.

The police officers who approached Eric see the matter very differently. They say they are protecting the rights of the people who live in Eric's neighborhood. It is a high-crime area. Most of the crimes there are committed by young males. The people who live there have a right to live safely. The police say that they can't prevent crime by waiting for it to happen. They need to stop it before it happens by making their presence known in the neighborhood. The police feel they are keeping the streets safe by aggressively seeking out potential crimes and criminals. They're only doing what the community wants.

In some ways, both Eric and the police officers are right. As citizens, Eric and his friends have certain rights, like being able to use public facilities peacefully. But the police officers have a duty to uphold those rights for everybody. They have to make sure that all citizens feel safe in their communities.

It is not always easy to tell just how far a citizen's rights should stretch. Sometimes both citizens and the police seem to overstep their limits. But just what are those limits? And how do we decide what the limits should be?

This book will try to answer those questions. It will look at some of the problems that occur when we try to determine just how much power the police should have. Most of us feel that as citizens we are free to do as we please, as long as we don't intrude on the rights of others. But the boundaries aren't always clear.

CONSTITUTIONAL RIGHTS

When America won its freedom from Great Britain, our Founding Fathers decided to write out a series of rules by which the new government would be run. These guidelines were called the Constitution. Our new government leaders also felt that the rights of citizens of the United States needed to be protected. They attached ten more guidelines, called amendments, to the Consti-

The Bill of Rights outlines how citizens are treated by the government, army and police.

tution. These amendments were called the *Bill of Rights*. The Bill of Rights set out how the government, army and police can treat individuals under the law.

Two of the ten amendments in the Bill of Rights are very important to our discussion of police, people and power. The *Fourth Amendment* guarantees people the right not to be searched or arrested without good reason. It says:

The right of the people to be secure in their persons, houses, papers and effects, against unreasonable searches and seizures, shall not be violated, and no warrants shall issue but upon probable cause, supported by oath or affirmation, and particularly describing the place to be searched, and the persons or things to be seized.

When making a criminal investigation, the police must show some evidence that the person they suspect is guilty of the crime. If they can show such *probable cause,* they will ask a judge for a *search warrant.* A search warrant allows the police to search a person's home or business for evidence. A search warrant is one way in which our rights are protected. If a police officer doesn't have one, he or she cannot legally collect evidence from your home. If an officer does conduct a search and collect evidence, and it is found that he or she didn't have the right to, then that evidence may not be used against you in court.

The *Fifth Amendment* is also very important to citizens' rights. It says that a person "shall not be compelled in any criminal case to be a witness against himself." This means that a person does not have to admit to a crime or provide police with evidence against himself.

"READ HIM HIS RIGHTS"

Throughout our history, many court cases between the police and citizens have tested the rights of both groups. One of the most important cases concerning the rights of citizens is the *Miranda* case. In the mid-1960s, a man named Ernesto Miranda was arrested for kidnap-

Court cases between the police and citizens have tested the rights of both groups.

ping and raping a woman in Phoenix, Arizona. At the police station, officers took Miranda to a special room where they interrogated him. After answering many questions, Miranda signed a paper that said he had voluntarily confessed to the crimes.

During his trial, Miranda was quickly found guilty. He was sentenced to 20 to 30 years in prison. After his conviction, Miranda's lawyer appealed the case. He asked that Miranda be set free because the police had violated his rights. They had not told Miranda that he did not have to answer questions that might incriminate him. They had not told Miranda about his Fifth Amendment right not to have to say things that might later lead to his conviction.

Miranda's case reached the U.S. Supreme Court—the highest court in the country. There, the Court agreed with Miranda's lawyer. They said that the police should have told Miranda of his rights and should have warned him that if he did say anything it could be used against him in court. They ordered that Miranda be retried. At this second trial, Miranda was again convicted, but because of other evidence, not his own admission of guilt.

The *Miranda* case is important to citizens' rights because it established specific guidelines for the way in which the police are permitted to deal with suspected criminals. You've probably heard a television cop reading *Miranda* rights to a suspect. Because of the Supreme Court's decision in *Miranda v. Arizona*, every suspected criminal must be made aware of his or her rights before being questioned. Here is what the police must say:

You have the right to remain silent. If you give up this right, anything you say can and will be used against you in a court of law. You have the right to have an attorney present at the time of your questioning. If you cannot afford an attorney, one will be appointed for you.

The *Miranda* case has been a very controversial one. Many people feel that *Miranda* rights are necessary. They say that people need to know what their rights are. Without this knowledge and protection, people might be intimidated by the police. *Miranda* rights keep things fair.

Other people argue that the *Miranda* decision gave too many rights to criminals. The police, they say, shouldn't be bothered by so many rules—especially where there is so much crime and so many dangerous criminals. The police are putting their lives on the line. They shouldn't have to worry about saying *Miranda* while arresting a gunman. Critics of *Miranda* point to another case, which occurred in 1980, as a perfect example of the problem with the *Miranda* warning.

In this case, two police officers approached a man named Benjamin Quarles. He fit the description of a suspected rapist. When Quarles saw the officers coming, he ran. The officers drew their guns and Quarles stopped.

The officers noticed that Quarles was wearing a gun holster. Before reading him his rights, one officer asked Quarles where his gun was. Quarles pointed to it.

At Quarles's trial, the judge disallowed much of the evidence against him. The judge said that Quarles's rights had been violated. He said that Quarles did not have to tell the officer where the gun was because the information would help convict him. Such an answer was self-incrimination.

Like the *Miranda* case, this case went to the Supreme Court. This time, the Court ruled that the police were allowed to ask Quarles about the gun. They said that the whereabouts of the gun posed a dangerous threat. The threat to the officers—and to the public—outweighed Quarles's rights.

Such exceptions to the *Miranda* rules make this "people and police" issue highly controversial and blur the line between the rights of police and the rights of citizens.

FORCING THE POINT

Anyone who watched television during the spring and summer of 1991 has a vivid memory of the way the police sometimes misuse their power. In March 1991 a citizen with a video recorder filmed five Los Angeles police officers beating an unarmed African-American

The incidents in Los Angeles and Fort Worth are unusual because they are documented on videotape.

man. His name was Rodney King. He had been asked to pull over because of a traffic violation. When he didn't pull over right away, the police followed him. Finally, King pulled over and got out of the car.

In the film, King is shown first on his feet and then on the ground. He offers no resistance as the officers beat him. In fact, King seems to be trying to shield himself from the blows. Many other police officers stand around watching as King is kicked and beaten by the officers with their nightsticks. King had to be hospitalized for his numerous injuries.

To most people who had seen the video tape, this was a clear case of police brutality. However, when the case finally went to trial in 1992, the police officers were found not guilty. Many people thought that since the jury did not contain any African Americans, the verdict was racially biased. Shortly after the verdict was reached, massive riots started in the streets of Los Angeles. Rioting soon spread to many other cities across the United States, causing a great deal of damage, as well as the loss of many lives.

Only a few months after the King incident, in July, another beating incident was videotaped. This time it was in Fort Worth, Texas. An officer was filmed beating a man with his nightstick. He struck him over two dozen times. The man was handcuffed at the time he was being beaten. The officer said that the man was a suspect in a car theft. He had been trying to escape from a moving police car. When the officer realized the suspect had tried to escape, he began to hit him.

The incidents in Los Angeles and Fort Worth are becoming well known as examples of what is called the use of *excessive force* by police officers in the apprehension of criminals. The officers used an amount of physical violence that was unnecessary and dangerous to the suspect. While the police argue that they must protect themselves from physical danger, others contend that too often the police use their weapons as an excessive means to "teach the bad guys a lesson."

WITNESS

Twenty-five-year-old Anton had thought a lot about these incidents. He remembered feeling shocked and angry as he saw the videotapes shown repeatedly on news programs. But he was even more surprised months later, when he actually witnessed a similar incident in his own neighborhood.

As he was moving his garbage cans to the curb one Thursday night, Anton looked across the street to a large apartment building. A police car was parked in front of the building. Two police officers were speaking to a teenager Anton recognized. The youth was one of many teenage boys who hung out in front of the building after school and on weekends.

As Anton stared across the street, he was startled to see one of the officers suddenly grab the teenager and throw him against the hood of the police car. The other officer then shoved him to the ground. Then, the two officers began kicking the youth.

Anton later remembered his shock as he watched the beating. "At first I thought the teenager must have a gun or something," he said. "I figured he must have done something really threatening. But then I realized he wasn't armed. And he wasn't fighting back, either."

As Anton watched, the officers stopped kicking the teenager and pulled him up from the pavement. Though the teen was obviously hurt and badly shaken up, he managed to stand on his feet while the officers got into their car and left. Anton ran across the street to see if he needed help. The boy was in some pain, but he insisted he was all right. Anton asked what happened. The boy just shrugged his shoulders.

"They're just trying to scare me, give me a warning," he said. "They were questioning me about some drug dealers in the neighborhood. I know who the dealers are, but I don't have anything to do with them. But do you think the police are going to believe that? Let's just forget it."

Anton watched in amazement as the boy began to walk slowly down the street. The witness didn't know what to do. Obviously, the police couldn't go around beating people up, even if they suspected them of a crime. But the teenager himself wasn't going to do anything about it.

And who can I tell? thought Anton. Usually, the police are the ones you call for help. Who do you call if the police are the ones who need to be reported? And, Anton thought bitterly, who's going to believe me? There were no other witnesses, and he felt sure the two police officers would deny it. He shook his head. If only I'd had a video camera, he thought to himself as he headed back home.

The other incidents, in Los Angeles and Fort Worth, are unusual because they are documented on videotape. There was evidence that the police abused their power.

These videotapes have raised questions about how and when police officers should use force. Sometimes the police are right to use it.

Police officers regularly find themselves in risky, even life-threatening, situations. They must deal with people who are hostile, unpredictable and very antagonistic toward police officers. Officers must always be prepared to protect themselves and other citizens as well. For this reason, they are allowed to use force to control a person when it is necessary. But deciding when force is necessary can be very difficult.

Police officers regularly find themselves in risky, life-threatening situations.

Police officers usually have only a few moments in which to make a decision about using force. Suspects may be acting irrationally, and their behavior may become violent very quickly. Officers may find themselves in the middle of angry confrontations. The suspect may be carrying or using weapons. If officers believe that their lives, or the lives of other citizens, may be in danger, they may use their own weapons.

A SHOT IN THE DARK

Such a decision was made by Officer Gary Neely. During a warm spring night, he and his partner were patrolling a quiet neighborhood. Suddenly they got a call about a van that had just been stolen by a group of teenagers a few blocks away. It was believed that one member of the group might be carrying a weapon.

Officer Neely and his partner began the chase. A few minutes later they had caught up to the van as it entered the freeway. After another couple of minutes of a dangerous, high-speed chase, the van exited the freeway, heading off to a quiet side street. Sirens wailing, the police car soon followed. They saw the van screech to a halt and three people jump out and begin running.

As the police car neared the van, Officer Neely pulled to a stop and jumped out of the car. While his partner stayed near the car, Officer Neely began running after the suspects. He yelled "Stop!" as loudly as he could, and then he fired a warning shot in the air. Two of the suspects, both young men, dived to the ground on a nearby lawn. The third slowed his pace as he ran behind a parked car. Then he began to turn toward the running Officer Neely.

That's when Officer Neely made his decision. According to the report he filed later, when he saw the third suspect move behind the parked car, he also thought he saw him reach into the jacket he was wearing. Officer Neely said that at that moment he believed that the suspect was reaching for a gun. He thought that if he hesitated, it could mean the loss of his own life. So he didn't hesitate. As the young man began to turn, Officer Neely fired three shots at him. In the next second, the young man fell to the ground.

One of the shots missed, hitting the car instead, but one hit the young man in the shoulder and one in the back. After the suspect was taken to the hospital, it was discovered that the last bullet had lodged in his spinal cord and would leave him paralyzed from the waist down. It was also discovered that the young man, an 18-year-old African-American named Barry Maxwell, wasn't carrying a weapon at all.

Many members of the community, as well as Maxwell's family, were outraged at the shooting. Though he had admitted to stealing the van, he had not, the family said, given Officer Neely sufficient reason to

Some citizens believe that police officers abuse their power. Others believe that officers are usually fair judges of a situation.

shoot him. He had not been carrying a gun, had not threatened anyone and had not posed a great danger to the police or to other citizens. Now he was being made to suffer permanently for being suspected of joyriding.

But Officer Neely said he believed the situation to be very dangerous. According to his statements, he had good reason to believe the suspect had a weapon, as he had been told over his car radio. Neely had fired a warning shot, and yelled "Stop," but Maxwell had kept running. And, the officer said, he didn't believe the teenagers were simply joyriding. The van had been stolen, and the teenagers, instead of pulling over right away, had led Officer Neely and his partner on a dangerous, high-speed chase. He believed that Maxwell posed a threat to his own safety and to that of other citizens.

Such incidents have made citizens nervous about the ways officers decide to use force. Some believe that a certain percentage of police officers are trigger-happy. They believe that some officers may automatically think the worst about a suspect, especially if he or she is a member of a minority group. The officers may not take the time to evaluate a situation properly before reacting with violence.

Others believe that officers are usually fair judges of a situation, especially considering that the situation is often dangerous. In a fast-moving, confusing chase or search, an officer must rely on instinct. If he or she hesitates, even for a few seconds, lives may be put in danger.

SUSPICIOUS MINDS

On a hot August night in 1990, 18-year-old Boyd Coombs left the garage where he worked and began walking toward an apartment complex a few blocks away. He had planned to drop in on a woman he had dated a few times. He had never been to her apartment, but he remembered that she had once told him where she lived. The two hadn't seen each other in a while, so Boyd had decided to surprise her with a visit.

But finding the apartment was more difficult than Boyd had expected. There were many small side streets in the area, and without a moon, the night was very dark. Boyd walked slowly past the large buildings, trying to get a glimpse of an address number or an owner's name.

Every citizen has the right not to be searched or arrested without good reason.

As he rounded a street corner, he suddenly heard the sound of screeching tires behind him. He turned around and was blinded by a huge searchlight aimed directly at his face. Covering his eyes, he could barely make out two men in suits running toward him. Boyd instinctively backed up a few steps, until he heard one of the men yell, "Don't move! Police!" In the next instant, he was face-to-face with the two men.

"What's going on?" Boyd asked, still covering his eyes.

Both men flashed their badges. "Good evening, sir," one of them said. "I'm Detective Lyons and this is Detective Schuller. We'd like to ask you a few questions."

"About what?" Boyd asked, feeling uncomfortable and confused.

"About what you're doing here," Detective Lyons said.

"I'm looking for my girlfriend's apartment," Boyd said, shrugging his shoulders.

The two detectives looked at each other. "Where does she live?" Detective Schuller asked.

Boyd shifted his feet a little. "I'm not really sure. She gave me directions, but I'm having a tough time getting my bearings around here."

"Why don't you just call her?" Detective Lyons asked suspiciously.

"Well, she doesn't exactly know I'm coming," Boyd said. What were all these questions for, anyway? he thought. "Look," he said, becoming impatient, "it's no crime to walk around the streets, right? What do you guys want?"

"What we want," Detective Schuller said slowly, "is to make sure that you are who you say you are. We'd simply like you to cooperate with us."

Boyd looked around in confusion. He felt like a criminal. The detectives kept looking at him as if he were on the FBI's "Most Wanted" list. Even though he didn't have anything to hide, he wasn't so sure he wanted to keep talking to the detectives. Can't a guy just walk down the street without being bothered?

As Boyd was to find out, the detectives weren't "bothering" him for no reason. They had been watching that area of town closely. A series of rapes had occurred in that vicinity over the last three months. They felt pretty sure that all of the rapes had been committed by the same person. The rapes had taken place in the same area, at the same time of night and by a man who was described almost identically by all of the victims. So the detectives had begun a heavy patrol of the neighborhood. They were on the lookout for any clues or any person who matched the description of the rapist.

And that's when Boyd came along. His height, weight and general appearance seemed similar to the alleged rapist's. He was walking alone, carefully looking at apartment buildings in the area where the rapes had occurred. And when his story about seeing his "girlfriend" seemed flimsy to the detectives, they decided to question him further at the police station.

Is it fair to stop a person for questioning just because he or she fits the description of a criminal?

For Boyd, who was merely minding his own business, the questioning seemed like a great imposition and a violation of his right to walk the streets. He was sorry for the victims. But being in the wrong place at the wrong time didn't necessarily make him a rape suspect.

The people who lived in the neighborhood, though, were glad to see the detectives actively trying to catch the rapist. Of course, the victims and their families didn't want the wrong man arrested. But in the effort to find the right man, they felt that Boyd should be willing to cooperate with the detectives. After all, if he wasn't the rapist, then he had nothing to worry about. The detectives would simply question him and let him go. It's worth bothering a few citizens, the victims felt, if it helps the police find the real criminal.

Sometimes honest mistakes are made, but innocent citizens can be more than just bothered. In the summer of 1991, police in New York City were looking for a man who had allegedly raped a woman and taken her wallet. The police thought the man would begin using her credit cards and her bankcard.

Eventually, the police thought that they had their man. They released a photo taken by a camera in an automatic teller machine at a bank. Police said that the man in the photo was the alleged rapist and that he was using his victim's bankcard to get cash from the machine. They released the photo in the hope of getting more information about the man.

But it turned out that the police had released the

wrong photo. The photo, which had appeared on the front page of local newspapers, was of a completely innocent New Yorker. He was a cabdriver whose family was shocked to see his photo appearing in connection with a rape case.

The police explained the mistake and apologized to the man. But although the cabdriver's innocence was emphasized in later news stories, many felt that he had nevertheless suffered unfairly. A simple case of mistaken identity can become potentially dangerous when criminal activity is involved.

An even more potentially dangerous case of mistaken identity involving police and an "innocent" man occurred a few years ago in Wellesley, Massachusetts. The case involved a basketball player named Dee Brown. Brown, an African-American, played for the Boston Celtics. He was planning to settle in the Wellesley area, a predominantly white neighborhood. One night police, responding to a bank-robbery call, ran up to Brown, who was in his car. They demanded that he get out and put his hands up. The police even pulled their guns.

Brown was obviously not the man the police were looking for. Though the police later apologized for their actions, critics faulted them for their tactics. Brown had not fit the description of the robber *at all,* except for the fact that he was black. They claimed that because Brown was a black man in a wealthy, white neighborhood the police jumped to the conclusion that he was involved in the crime. They said that approaching a man simply because of the color of his skin is an act of prejudice.

MAKING A MOVE: POLICE INTERVENTION

Sometimes the police know that they should interfere but are not given the power to do it. Jameson Randall has been a police officer for eight years. He has chased down murderers, had gunfights with drug dealers and confronted burglars. But he says the stories that make the headlines are not always the most challenging ones. Sometimes, Randall says, it is the common, everyday situations among citizens that can be the trickiest for police officers.

For example, Randall and his partner answered a call from a frantic woman. The woman told the police dispatcher that her husband was drunk and had hit her. She was afraid he might explode with rage and seriously hurt her. Randall and his partner hurried to the address the dispatcher gave them.

But when they arrived, the woman met them at the door in a fairly calm manner. "Thank you for stopping by," she said quickly to the officers, "but everything is

Sometimes small arguments escalate to dangerous levels.

fine now. You can go." Randall remembers feeling confused and a little skeptical. After all, just a few minutes before, the woman had been almost hysterical, afraid of a drunk and dangerous husband. Now she was standing in front of them with a red, puffy cheek and claiming there was no problem.

"Are you sure you're all right, ma'am?" Randall asked politely.

"Yeah, I'm fine," the woman said, hiding her face. "We had an argument, and he just made me so mad that I called you guys. But it's fine now. He's already falling asleep. I don't want to press charges or anything."

It was a frustrating moment for Randall and his partner. They felt that the woman had been in real danger. She had been crying and was injured. And they felt that if her husband actually had abused her this time, there was a good chance he could do it again. Maybe she was just too scared of him to report the abuse. The officers wanted to prevent any future violence. If the woman would only let them, they could get help for her.

But right now, they did not know the whole story. As long as the woman didn't want them to investigate, they couldn't simply burst into her home, arrest her husband and begin interrogating him. There were no other witnesses, and the woman's report was all they had to go on. Even though they were suspicious, the police officers had to be careful about maintaining the rights of these citizens.

For Randall and other police officers, such situations

are common. They often have to determine how and when to intervene. Police officers must decide how to balance the need to protect one citizen with the right of another citizen not to be unnecessarily bothered. And often those decisions must be made very quickly.

For example, the police might get a call about a group of teenagers who are "disturbing the peace" at night. Neighbors might complain that the kids, who are hanging out on the sidewalk, are being too loud. But the kids may claim that they're only talking and that they are not out past their curfew. The police must then decide how they can intervene. They must weigh the needs of the neighbors, who want a peaceful neighborhood, and the teenagers, who want to use public areas to meet.

In the summer of 1991, police in New York City were called in to intervene in a situation in Tompkins Square Park. The small neighborhood park had become a home for many homeless people. They felt they had nowhere else to go, and they had set up permanent tents in certain sections of the park.

Some people in the neighborhood surrounding the park began to complain about the homeless camp in the park. They felt that as taxpaying citizens, they had a right to use all sections of the park. Now they were uncomfortable using the areas with the tents. And they were upset about the litter and waste generated by the homeless.

As the conflict between both sides increased, the

mayor of New York City ordered the police to move the homeless out of the park. Once again, the police had to intervene in a difficult situation. They became the targets of both outrage and appreciation as they forced the homeless to take their few belongings and leave the park. In this, as in other situations, trying to balance the rights of both groups inevitably led to some frustration and dissatisfaction.

Sections of Tompkins Square Park in New York City were once home to many homeless people. Eventually, the police had to force the homeless people to leave.

DISCRIMINATION: "BUT HE FITS THE DESCRIPTION"

As the police try to balance their need to stop crime with the rights guaranteed to citizens by the Constitution, they sometimes overstep their bounds in not so obvious ways. By using computers and statistics to tell them who commits crimes, the police very often anticipate what type of person is a criminal. Unfortunately, very often they are wrong.

Thirty-two-year-old Roger Williams, an African-American, had just arrived at the Los Angeles airport. A pro basketball player, Williams was hurrying to practice after missing the team flight from New York. Well dressed and carrying expensive luggage, Williams ran through the airport to catch a taxi.

As he sped through the crowded terminal, two plain-clothes police officers yelled for him to stop. "Freeze!" they yelled. "Drop your bags and put your hands up!" Williams did what he was told. He asked the police officers why he was being stopped. Finally, one of the officers said, "We want to search your bags. We're looking for suspected drug smugglers." Williams remained calm, but he was angry. "Look," he said, "I'm Roger Williams, the basketball player. I'm no drug dealer. You have no right to do this," he continued, his voice rising a bit.

Police officers frequently use computers to compile crime statistics.

"Oh yes we do," said one of the officers as he looked through Williams's luggage.

With all the commotion, a crowd was gathering around Williams and the police officers. Williams was now furious, repeating his statement that he was "no drug dealer." The quick search produced nothing. The officers looked at Williams's identification and apologized for what they called a "misunderstanding."

"You fit the description of our drug dealer profile," said the second officer.

"You mean because I'm black and well dressed, it means I'm a drug dealer," countered Williams. "Well, I think that's discrimination, and your police force will be hearing from my attorneys. You can't just stop someone because of the way they look."

Situations like Williams's are not uncommon. In fact, police and federal agencies do use the method of *profiling* to try to identify likely criminals. Their officers stop all those people who fit the descriptions. Many times they stop and embarrass innocent people. Critics of this police tactic argue that it is discriminatory and prejudicial. By creating a profile of a drug dealer who is young, black and well dressed, the police are creating an image, a *stereotype,* that all young, wealthy blacks are criminals. These critics want to ban the use of profiling to stop and search anybody who fits the general description.

One famous case brought much negative attention to this police technique. Joe Morgan, a famous ex-baseball player, was stopped by airport police in just this manner. He was humiliated in front of a large crowd because he "fit the description" of a drug smuggler.

Critics argue that there are many ways in which the police discriminate against particular groups of people. Age, race and wealth all play a part. Teenagers are often singled out as criminals just because they are "hanging out" with nothing to do.

Minority groups contend that they receive less help from the police than other, more accepted groups. In

Brooklyn, New York, Hispanic and black communities continually complain that the police treat the richer—and whiter—Jewish communities better.

Many gay communities say the same thing. They say that the police aren't quick to investigate harassment and assault charges brought by homosexuals because the officers are prejudiced against them. Unfortunately, such accusations are hard to prove. And the general perception that the police don't do enough to protect all groups equally is just as hard to erase.

For many, images of blatantly discriminatory practices by the police are difficult to forget. During the 1950s and 1960s, southern blacks were protesting to end racial discrimination in the South. Police were filmed using vicious police dogs and powerful fire hoses to subdue the protesters. Peaceful marchers in Mississippi and Alabama were beaten with nightsticks. This treatment got so bad in Alabama that President Lyndon Johnson was forced to call out the National Guard to protect the rights of these protesters.

Police officers accused of lynching blacks were often supported and applauded by their communities. Rather than feeling protected by the police, many blacks felt threatened by anyone in a police uniform. Today, while there is a general outcry against such violently prejudicial practices, many feel that discrimination is still widespread.

Teenagers are often singled out as troublemakers because they are "hanging out" with nothing to do.

HERE WE GO AGAIN: SYSTEMATIC HARASSMENT

Edgar Clark is 53 years old. For the last two years he has been living in a smattering of blankets under an old bridge. After losing his job and his apartment four years ago, he moved from shelter to shelter, finally ending up under the bridge. He collects old furnishings that people have thrown out. He gets food where he can—garbage cans, soup kitchens or what he can buy with the money he finds.

Edgar's life doesn't sound very easy or hopeful to most people. But Edgar says he doesn't want sympathy and doesn't want to complain. What he does want, he says, is to be left alone by the police. According to Edgar, he is harassed all the time. If he falls asleep on a park bench, he is awakened by a cop and told to move along. If he sits inside the bus station to eat his lunch, a cop usually comes along to ask him to leave. If he sits on the sidewalk to rest, a cop will approach him to ask him what he's doing.

Edgar says he never bothers people and is not a criminal. He thinks he is perpetually harassed simply because he looks different. His ragged and dirty appearance makes people uncomfortable and suspicious. So no matter where he goes, he says, the police are always there, asking questions or making "requests" of him.

Many of the police officers in Edgar's community know him by name. They have tried to get him a permanent shelter, and they say they don't deliberately harass him. The officers say they get a lot of complaints about him, and it's their job to check out those complaints. With business owners, store workers and parents always

Systematic harassment occurs when certain people are constantly bothered by the police because they have questionable reputations.

nagging them to do something, they have no choice but to keep watch over Edgar.

But some people say that the police treatment of Edgar is just one example of *systematic harassment*. Certain groups in society are constantly bothered by the police because they have questionable reputations. Beggars or homeless people, teenagers, homosexuals and others say that they have been made targets of the police. They say they are more likely than other citizens to be suspected of crimes and to be questioned by police. They are not allowed the freedoms other citizens have because their actions are always interpreted suspiciously.

Of course, it is illegal to harass people simply because of their race, occupation, sexual preference or appearance. But many of these groups claim that their relationships with the police is different than those of other citizens'. They feel the police basically try to work against them, rather than protect them.

They may feel they are actually sought out by police, who then use subtle means to intimidate them. Officers may be sarcastic or taunting when speaking to certain citizens. They may carry two sets of handcuffs, or wear mirrored sunglasses, trying to look the part of a tough, macho cop. Members of the targeted groups say that such officers are nothing more than bullies and give a bad name to the police force as a whole.

WORKING WITH THE COMMUNITY

Minority groups are not the only ones who are annoyed by bullying police tactics. Members of the police force themselves often complain that a few power-hungry officers can give the whole force a bad reputation in the community. Many officers say that while most members of the force are careful to follow standard regulations and procedures, there are always a handful of officers who want to flaunt their authority. Those are the officers, they say, who are responsible for making the community distrustful of, and even hostile toward, all police officers.

Recently, police departments have started programs to deal with officers who continually abuse their power. In the past, many departments were criticized for not properly punishing officers who ignore regulations. It was said that a police officer would never turn in a fellow officer, even for blatant wrongdoings. Today, in some cities, steps are being taken to make sure all officers are held responsible for their actions.

In Kansas City, Missouri, for example, officers with unusually large numbers of complaints against them are singled out. The new police chief has introduced educational programs and penalties for those officers who

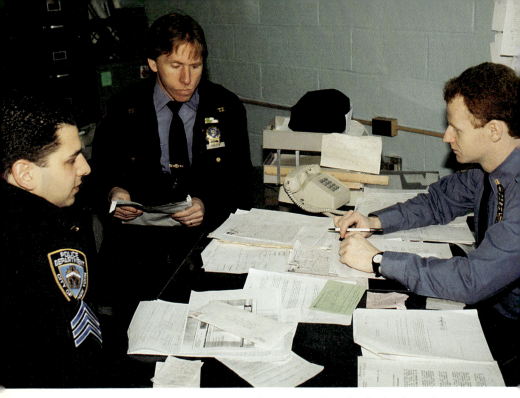

New York City's police department tries to monitor the behavior of its officers.

seem to abuse their authority. The officers are taught new ways to handle common police situations.

New York City's police department has also introduced a new plan to monitor, or watch, the possibly harassing or brutal behavior of its officers. Like the Kansas City program, New York City's plan includes counseling for officers. But officers who receive a lot of complaints against them are investigated by a special police task force, called the Internal Affairs Division. If found guilty of brutality charges, officers will be dismissed.

Unfortunately, critics of police forces say that the police do not watch, or punish, themselves well enough. They argue that despite what police departments say, very few officers are punished for brutal behavior. A newspaper survey conducted in 1991 found that only 2 percent of the New York Police Department officers charged with brutality were punished. Very often, the police don't want to tell on their buddies. So, charges of brutality are usually only the citizen's word against the officer's. And, when other government agencies try to investigate brutality charges, the police often don't cooperate.

Police departments across the country still say that there are only a few bad cops out there. They say that to build a better image and make improvements in policing, officers need the cooperation of the community. Many departments have set up community-assistance groups. Members of the community form groups that try to aid the police in their work. Teen patrols, community councils and neighborhood-watch programs have all been established with the help of their local police departments. In addition, police departments have tried to work with communities on a less formal basis by sponsoring community events, setting up sports programs for kids or meeting with members of a neighborhood to hear complaints.

And both police and citizens' groups say that one of the best ways to help a community is to be a watchful citizen. Witnesses are often the most important part of

Many police departments sponsor community events such as sports programs for kids.

any questionable incident. Without third-party accounts of a situation, it can be very difficult to settle disputes between police and citizens, and between citizens themselves. When members of a community are willing to speak up and willing to get involved, a dispute has a much better chance of being resolved fairly.

FOR MORE INFORMATION

For more information on citizens' rights, you can contact:

American Civil Liberties Union
132 West 43d Street
New York, NY 10036
(212) 944-9800

GLOSSARY/INDEX

BILL OF RIGHTS 8—*The first ten amendments to the U.S. Constitution, which establish certain citizens' rights.*

EXCESSIVE FORCE 15—*The physical violence used by police that is unnecessary and dangerous to a suspect.*

FIFTH AMENDMENT 9, 11—*The amendment that guarantees citizens the right not to have to give evidence against themselves.*

FOURTH AMENDMENT 8—*The amendment that guarantees people the right not to be searched or arrested without good reason.*

***MIRANDA* RIGHTS** 11, 12, 13—*Rights that must be read to a criminal suspect when he or she is being arrested.*

PROBABLE CAUSE 9—*Some form of evidence that police present to a judge when trying to get a search warrant against a particular suspect.*

PROFILING 37—*A police technique in which a general description of a type of criminal is created in order to spot and stop that type.*

SEARCH WARRANT 9—*A court order that allows police to search a particular place for evidence of criminal activity.*

STEREOTYPE 37—*An overly general mental picture of a person, usually based on broad characteristics of the person's background.*

SYSTEMATIC HARASSMENT 42—*The continual questioning and pestering of certain groups of citizens by the police.*